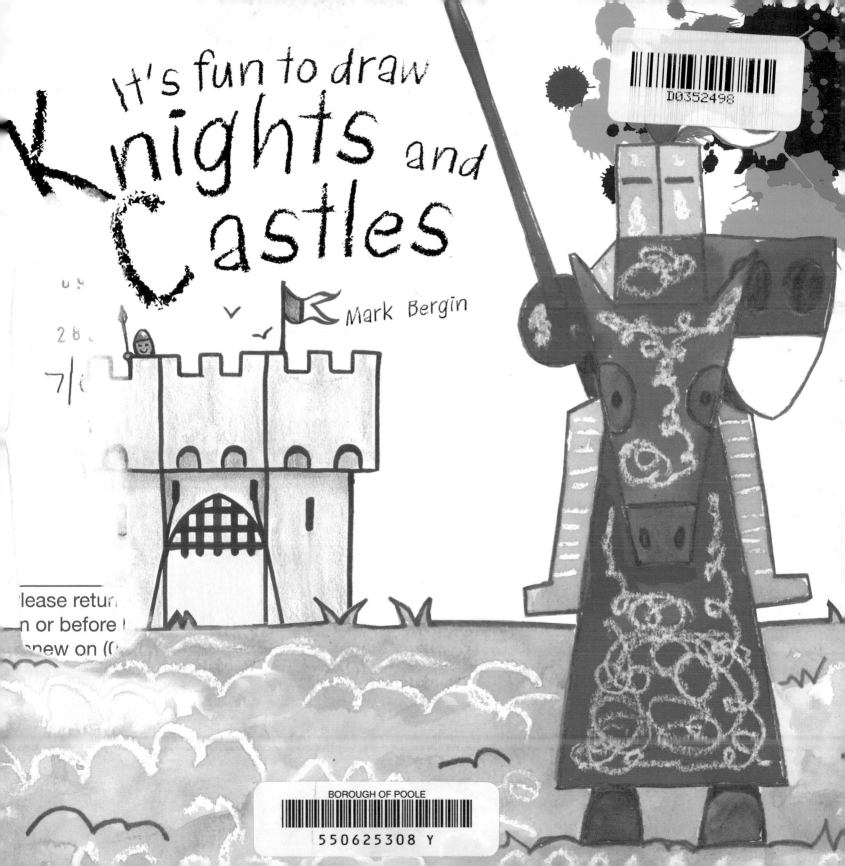

It's fun to draw
Knights and Castles

Mark Bergin

Author:
Mark Bergin was born in Hastings, England.
He has illustrated an award-winning series and
written over twenty books. He has done many book
designs, layouts and storyboards in many styles
including cartoon for numerous books, posters and
adverts. He lives in Bexhill-on-Sea with his wife
and three children.

Editorial Assistant:
Rob Walker

HOW TO USE THIS BOOK:

Start by following the numbered splats on the left
hand page. These steps will ask you to add some
lines to your drawing. The new lines are always
drawn in red so you can see how the drawing builds
from step to step. Read the 'You can do it!' splats
to learn about drawing and colouring techniques
you can use.

Published in Great Britain in MMXII by
Book House, an imprint of
The Salariya Book Company Ltd
25 Marlborough Place, Brighton BN1 1UB
www.salariya.com
www.book-house.co.uk

ISBN-13: 978-1-907184-70-3

A CIP catalogue record for this book is available
from the British Library.

Printed and bound in China.

PAPER FROM
SUSTAINABLE
FORESTS

Visit our website at **www.book-house.co.uk**
or go to **www.salariya.com** for **free** electronic versions of:
You Wouldn't Want to be an Egyptian Mummy!
You Wouldn't Want to be a Roman Gladiator!
You Wouldn't Want to be a Polar Explorer!
You Wouldn't Want to Sail on a 19th-Century Whaling Ship!

Visit our BookHouse100 channel to see Mark Bergin doing
step by step illustrations:

www.youtube.com/user/bookhouse100

Contents

4   Castle guard

6   Eagleford Castle

8   Norman knight

10   Axe knight

12   Archer

14   Ravenswood Castle

16   Jousting tent

18   Jousting knight

20   The joust

22   Mace knight

24   Hawkbury Castle

26   Arabian knight

28   Spearman

30   Battling knight

32   Index

Castle guard

1 Start with the helmet. Add eye slots and dots for breathing holes.

2 Add a shield. Draw in markings.

you can do it!
Use a black felt-tip for the lines and add colour using watercolour paint.

3 Draw a rectangle for the body and add legs.

4 Add the arm holding a spear.

5 Draw in a belt and a scabbard.

splat-a-fact!
Important knights lived in castles.

Eagleford Castle

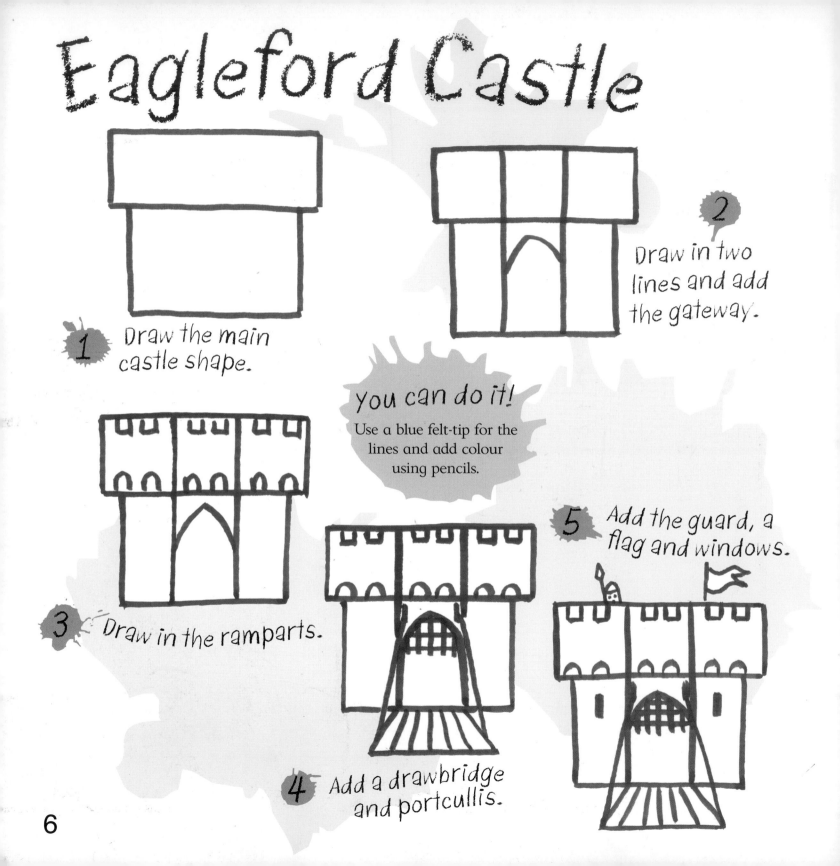

1 Draw the main castle shape.

2 Draw in two lines and add the gateway.

you can do it!

Use a blue felt-tip for the lines and add colour using pencils.

3 Draw in the ramparts.

4 Add a drawbridge and portcullis.

5 Add the guard, a flag and windows.

Norman knight

1 Start with the shield.

2 Add the tunic.

3 Draw in the head with a mouth and a dot for the eye. Add a pointed helmet.

you can do it!
Use wax crayons for the colour and a black felt-tip for the lines.

4 Draw in an arm holding a sword.

5 Add the legs.

9

Axe knight

1 Cut out a helmet. Draw a slit and breathing holes. Stick down onto coloured paper.

2 Cut out a tunic from yellow paper. Stick down.

3 Now tear out the shield shape and stick down. Tear out a red cross and add to shield.

splat-a-fact!
Knights could fight with an axe or just throw it at the enemy.

you can do it!
Cut out the knight's armour shapes from tin foil. Use a marker pen for the details.

4 Cut out legs. Stick down. Add detail.

5 Cut out an arm and the axe head. Cut out the handle. Stick down. Add details.

MAKE SURE YOU GET AN ADULT TO HELP YOU WHEN USING SCISSORS!

Archer

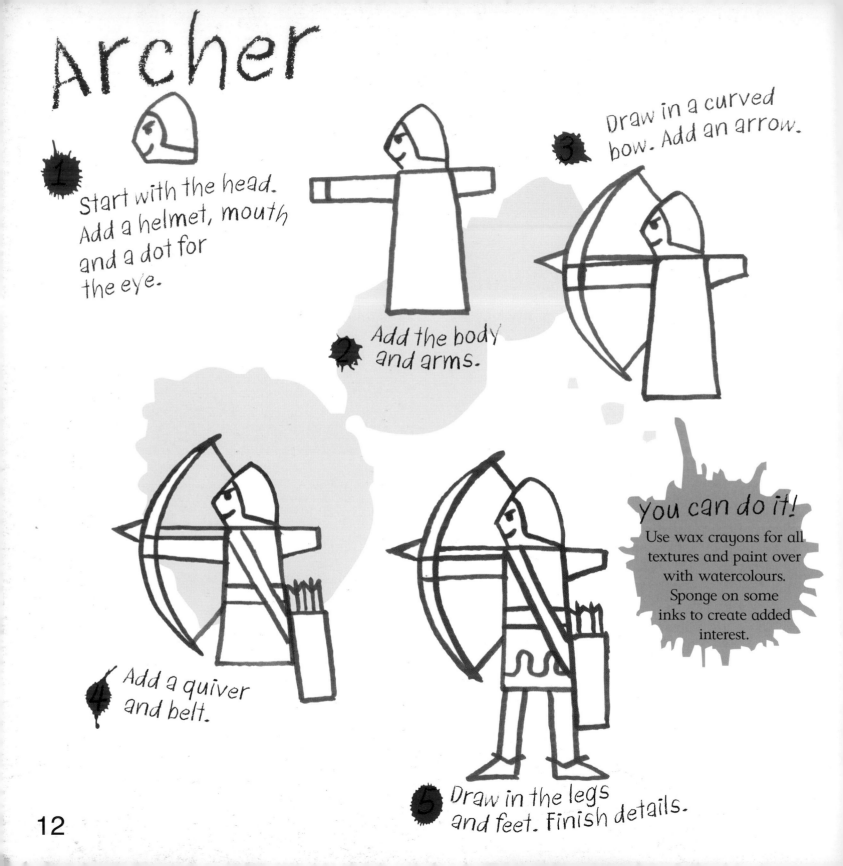

1 Start with the head. Add a helmet, mouth and a dot for the eye.

2 Add the body and arms.

3 Draw in a curved bow. Add an arrow.

4 Add a quiver and belt.

5 Draw in the legs and feet. Finish details.

you can do it! Use wax crayons for all textures and paint over with watercolours. Sponge on some inks to create added interest.

Archers stood on top of battlements and shot at the enemy.

13

Ravenswood Castle

1 Start with a square and add a gateway.

2 Draw in the towers and add windows.

you can do it!

Use a soft pencil for the lines and add colour using watercolour paint.

splat-a-fact!

The main gate was very strong. It was a thick, iron-studded, wooden door.

3 Draw in triangles for the pointed roofs.

4 Add finishing details: windows, doors and battlements.

14

Jousting tent

1 Start with the tent top. Add a wavy line.

2 Draw in the tent with a gap for the entrance.

you can do it!
Use a black felt-tip for the lines and add colour using coloured felt-tips.

splat-a-fact!
The knight's jousting tent was where he got ready for the tournament.

3 Add stripes and a flag.

4 Draw the knight's colours on the flag and banner.

Jousting knight

1

Start with the horse's head and body.

you can do it!

Use wax crayons for all textures and paint over with watercolour paint. Use a pencil for the lines.

2 Add the eyes, nostrils and hooves.

3

Draw in the knight with a helmet. Add his legs either side of the horse.

4 Add a lance and shield. Draw feathers on the helmet.

splat-a-fact!

It took about 14 years to train to be a knight.

The joust

1 Start with the horse's head and surcoat.

2 Add its eyes, mouth, tail and hooves.

you can do it!
Use a brown felt-tip for the lines and add colour with coloured felt-tips.

3 Draw in the knight with a shield.

4 Draw in the reins and a saddle. Add detail to the surcoat.

5 Add a lance and a feather on the helmet.

splat-a-fact!
A knight needed lots of money - a shiny suit of armour was very expensive.

Mace knight

1 Start with the helmet shape. Add a visor with dots for breathing holes and two slits for the eyes.

2 Add the knight's tunic and shield.

Splat-a-fact!

A knight wore his 'colours' on his tunic and shield to show who was inside the suit of armour.

3 Add a belt and the legs.

4 Draw in the arm holding a mace.

you can do it!

Use coloured pencils and a black felt-tip for the lines. Smudge or blend the colour for more interest.

Hawkbury Castle

1 Cut out the middle section of the castle. Stick down.

2 Cut out two towers. Stick down.

You can do it!

Cut out the shapes from coloured paper. Stick these on to a sheet of blue paper. Use felt-tip for the lines.

3 Draw in windows and a doorway.

4 Add a guard and a large banner on top.

MAKE SURE YOU GET AN ADULT TO HELP YOU WHEN USING SCISSORS!

splat-a-fact!
The walls of a castle are very high to stop attackers climbing in.

25

Arabian knight

1 Start with the tunic and a round shield. Add details.

2 Add the head, with dots for the eyes, a nose and a moustache.

3 Add the helmet shape.

you can do it!
Use wax crayons to create textures and paint over with watercolour paint. Use a soft pencil for the lines.

4 Draw in an arm holding a curved sword.

5 Add the scabbard. Draw in the legs.

Arabian knights had to fight in the desert. It was important that they had water to drink between battles.

27

spearman

1

Start with the
helmet and the head.
Add dots for the
eyes and a mouth.

2

Add the tunic.

3

Draw in the
arm and spear.

you can do it!

Use a brown felt-tip for the lines
and add colour with soft, chalky
pastels. Smudge and blend some
of the colours to add interest.

splat-a-fact!

In battle, the spearman
could keep enemies at a
safe distance with his
long spear.

4 Add a long
shield shape.

5

Draw in the legs.

Battling knight

1 Start with the helmet. Add slits for the eyes and a pointed beak shape.

2 Add a shield with a cross.

3 Draw in a belted tunic with a cross on it.

you can do it!

Use wax crayons for texture and paint over it with watercolour paint. Use felt-tip for the lines.

4 Draw in the legs wearing armour.

5 Add an arm holding a sword aloft.

splat-a-fact!

A knight's suit of armour had to be built to fit him exactly.

Index

A
Arabian 26, 27
archer 12, 13
axe 10, 11

B
banner 16, 24
battlements 12, 14
Battle of Hastings, The 8

C
castle 4, 6, 7, 14, 24, 25

D
drawbridge 6, 7

F
felt-tip 4, 6, 8, 16, 20, 22, 24, 28, 30
flag 6, 16

G
gateway 6, 14
guard 4, 6, 24

H
helmet 4, 8, 10, 12, 18, 20, 22, 26, 28, 30
horse 18-21

J
jousting 16, 18-21

M
mace 22, 23

N
Norman 8

P
pastels 28
pencil 6, 14, 18, 22, 26

S
scabbard 4, 26
shield 4, 8, 10, 12, 18, 20, 22, 26, 28, 30
spear 4, 28, 29
surcoat 20, 21
sword 8, 26, 27, 30, 31

T
tower 14, 24
tunic 8, 10, 22, 26, 28, 30

W
watercolour 4, 12, 14, 18, 26, 30
wax crayons 8, 12, 18, 26, 30

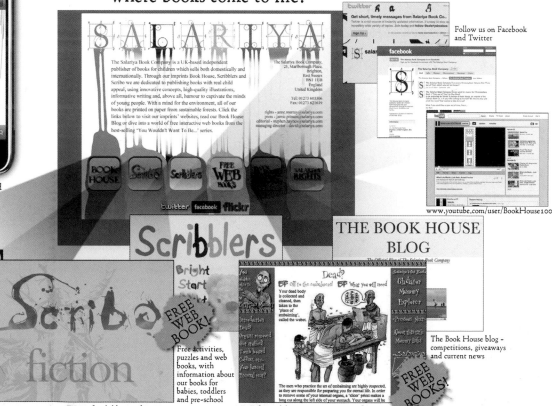
iPhone and iPad are registered trademarks of Apple Inc.